I Pray, Immanuel

A Supplement Devotional to
A Teacher's Prayer
by: Tammy Mentzer Brown

ISBN **978-1-935786-47-4**

Printed in the United States of America
St. Clair Publications
P. O. Box 726
Mc Minnville, TN 37111-0726
http://stclairpublications.com

Cover Design by Kent Hesselbein
© 2013 KGH Design Studio
http://www.kghdesignstudio.com/services.html

INTRODUCTION:

Format of Class

- Supplies needed: Bible and optional, A Teacher's Prayer, by Tammy Mentzer Brown (available at http://.stclairpublications.com or www.amazon.com)
- Each session will include searching of scripture, completing devotional guide and potential reading of three to five chapters per session out of the book, A Teacher's Prayer.
- If you are participating in small group time, it will include: prayer, guided discussion of handouts (Assignments for Reflection) and reading when applicable, and Class Segment for upcoming week. If you are not participating in a small group, this study can still be used as a devotional, including the class work segment of each session.

This study is designed for us to seek guidance on our calling as Christians and to better understand our impact on others, while enhancing our personal relationship with Christ.

Each Session begins with a "list sheet" to use as a resource for goals in this study. Please take time to complete it.

Letter from the Author:

Dear Participant:

I will be praying that you will find some sense of a deeper connection with God during this study, as well as an opportunity to bond and familiarize yourself with your fellow group of believers. Immanuel, God with us, is a powerful truth and sentiment that if we would purposely seek each morning when we awake; we might marvel at just how much God can use us daily! While this study can be completed independently, I believe you will find it more of a blessing in a small group setting; because there is something extra special when we gather together in God. For those genuinely curious about the message of the book, it is important to know this is my personal testimony and a calling to share how God can use each of us in various situations to make the world a better place for any one given person. I have grown a very fond understanding that God did choose each of us. I also realize that more times than not, we get too busy to remember and/or realize just how much He wants to use us for His glory. Revelation 12:6 states, "They overcame him by the blood of the Lamb and the word of their testimony." Therefore take time to remember how and why you started serving Christ then seek for Him to use you even more as His witness here on earth!

I pray, Immanuel,

Tammy

Prayer Line for whom this week:

This is the section you can list prayer request in.

> Take time to remember these requests every time you sit down to work on your devotionals. Make it a habit to start at the beginning of each session's devotion and remember your prayer requests...then pray for God to bless these requests and your study!

Times set aside for God this week:

If you are goal oriented, schedule yourself a time for study; or track it and see how much time you are spending with God!

> Do you write lesson plans or agendas or calendar dates in for things to remember what you have coming up? What about tracking your exercise or diet or spending habits? Most of us do and we do it for accountability. Try tracking your study time! When you write it, you focus more on accomplishing it.

Who needs a note this week?

A simple hand written note is such a commodity of endearment that we have gotten away from since technology has advanced us so.

> Find a friend, neighbor, teacher, service member or family, shut-in, resident of a nursing home or children's home or anyone that could use cheer! Try to write at least one a week, but wow, if you could do more! Just commit to it during this study. You have no clue how much a hand written note means-even from a stranger! I do! ☺

Scripture:

Memorize your scripture

> Take this section to write in your scripture for the lesson. Maybe even write it on a note card each week and put it somewhere you will remember to read it over and over until it is tucked in your heart permanently. You never know when you will need it!

Session I~KINDNESS

Prayer Line for whom this week:

Times set aside for God this week:

Total Time	Date & Day

Who needs a note this week?

Name	Address

Scripture for the week: Psalms 90:12

Date:_____

NOTES /JOURNAL

SESSION I ~ KINDNESS

Reading

A Teacher's Prayer – Chapters 1-5
Bible passages outlined in Assignment for Reflection

Class Segment

A typical day starts with a sunrise and ends with a sunset, but the way we welcome that view is completely up to us. Choose the one most like you:

_____ The light is too bright and I tug fast at the blanket to cover my eyes to shield myself for another few minutes of rest.

_____ I toss the covers aside, rise from bed, and begin the day with a smile to welcome another day to enjoy.

_____ Neither of the above—I am routine enough that the covering of my eyes is not necessary, the joy of celebrating a new day does not enter my mind first thing in the morning and I begin with waking to the alarm clock reminding me it is yet another day of routine: get out of bed, make it to the bathroom to shower, wash my face and dress and then to the kitchen for that cup of coffee before hastily scurrying the family to school and work.

The good news is there is no right or wrong answer. We each respond differently to everything we do. See our God doesn't focus on the legalities of what we do, but the reason we do it—our heart—if you will. My hope during this study is for you to take time and look at your day to day life and your focus in it. For your assignment, you will be asked to dig into scripture to search out some direction in your Christian walk. Please set aside a little time each day to complete the assignments so that you can come back together as a class and have meaningful discussions; however do not skip the class if you miss the assignments, because you can still receive a blessing just by being there!

Now turn to Psalms 90:12 and write in, on your list page, this passage (sheet prior).

Beginning Prayer: Dear God, cleanse my heart and teach me to call on You to help me number my days, understanding that each and every day You can use me to make a difference!

Assignment for Reflection

Discuss these two questions. 1. What chain of events brought you to your present walk with Christ? 2. What actions of others first initiated those steps?

1._____

_____

2._____

_____

Usually our Christian walk starts out with good intentions because we are so excited about what God has done, so much so, we are willing to share with others. As time goes by our schedules change, our responsibilities towards personal relationships change, and demands on our time change. As the stresses of life blur our focus and diminish our enthusiasm, we need to take time to stop and inventory our spiritual walk, by looking at where we are as well as why we are here.

In my story, I share an example of being invited to Vacation Bible School at age seven. It was there God would take time through fun and food to bring me back day after day to hear His story. This was made possible, because a man followed God's lead and invited a widow's children to VBS that summer. It was there at VBS that I would come to receive an unshakeable foundation in my life of hope for a better life and a better me. That is how it all began for me. If you have not yet revisited your roots to your walk with God above, please go back and do that now.

No one's story is complete without telling how the story began. The great news is that I believe no one's story is ever over—there really is no end. And do you know why? When we hear a really good story, we do not want it to end-do we? A great movie or book—we want a sequel. God's story is that good and you are that sequel! Have you ever thought about this? How do you think your life is a sequel to Christ coming into your life?

_____

_____

_____

_____.

If we look back to the people that showed us the way to the Lord or even to the Lord Himself and His disciples, who helped to spread that word, we will find that the story never ends. It continues to impact us and shape us today. That it was intended for us to be His sequel, to carry on His story and continue writing it. So how are you writing the life of your story? Just think about this to yourself for a moment. I know that sometimes we get too busy to remember everything and that is why we are going to focus on the topic of remembrance this week. You are a sequel to Christ in that He wants to use you to continue His story.

Draw on the scale below to represent your willingness to look for opportunities to share God with others consciously and deliberately daily. On a scale of 1-7, use 1 as not as likely and 7 as highly likely. First draw a circle to represent your willingness now then draw a triangle to represent your willingness when you first came to serve the Lord.

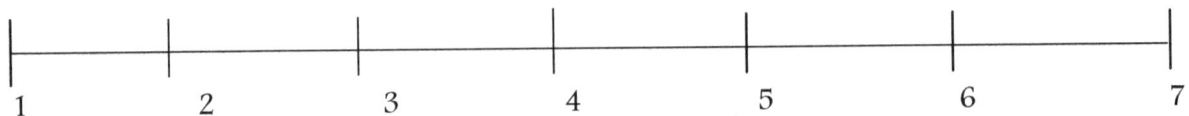

```
|————|————|————|————|————|————|
1     2     3     4     5     6     7
```

The reason to stop and consider your walk today versus when you first decided to follow Christ is, it is always meaningful to get back to our roots, to remember where we have come from. It was common for Israelites to remember events and celebrations in history because it was very inspirational to remember how much God accomplished and what He had promised them was yet to come. Can you list any feasts or festivals mentioned in the Bible?

_____

_____

_____

Use the following table[1] for more help on this topic:

Feast	OT Reference	Purpose	NT Prophetic Reference
Passover	Ex 12:1-28, 43-49	To remember Yahweh delivering Israel from bondage in Egypt as well as sparing their firstborn.	Matt 26:17-30 -foundation for the Lord's Supper; John 1:29, 19:36, 1 Cor 5:7, 1 Pet 1:18-19-Christ as our Passover
Feast of Unleavened Bread	Ex 12:15-20; 13:3-10	A symbol of devotion to God and consecration as well as to commemorate the hardships of the Exodus flight from Egypt	John 6:30-59 - represents Christ 1 Cor 5:7-8 represents the true church
Day of Firstfruits	Lev 23:9-14	Dedication of firstfruits of the barley harvest	1 Cor 5:20-23 - Symbolic of Christ's resurrected body 1 Cor 15:20-23; 1 Thess 4:13-18- Symbolic of the resurrection of believers
Feast of Pentecost	Ex 23:16; Lev 23:15-22	Dedication of firstfruits of the wheat harvest	Holy Spirit outpouring on the Day of Pentecost on the church
Day of Trumpets	Lev 23:23-25	7th month was consecrated as the sabbatical month	Matt 24:31, 1 Cor 15:42; 1 Thess 4:16- Associated with the return of Christ and the blowing of the trumpet
Day of Atonement	Lev 15:1-24	Annual atonement of the priest and the tabernacle of meeting	Crucifixion of Christ is the ultimate fulfillment for Atonement
Feast of Tabernacles	Lev 23:33-43 Num 10:10, 29:1-6	To remember Yahweh's protection and deliverance during the Exodus	Zech 14:16 - Foreshadowing of the millennial reign of Jesus kingdom of peace and prosperity through Him

Can you list any we hold today in remembrance of the Lord?

_____

_____

Remembering is just as important in our culture today. It usually holds true when looking at Christmas, births, weddings or funerals.

So, why remember? We remember to learn from, to celebrate, and to hope for things to come. When you get down to it, remembering can bring pain and joy, but it is on those positive memories that we can draw on the 'whys' of how it all began. Therefore we need to focus on

---

[1] The Woman's Study Bible, 2nd Edition, NKJV, Thomas Nelson, 1995, 2006, The Feasts of Israel, p 109

the 'why' we started our faith walk in the first place, so that we can appreciate where God wants to take us.

Meditate on this scripture: Psalms 90:12 and copy it down in the space below. Immediately following the verse, summarize what it means to you.

_____

_____

_____

_____

_____

_____

_____

_____

This Psalm was included as a passage of complaint in a time of distress. The Psalmist is crying out to be reminded that each day is a gift from God and should be lived in God. In God there is wisdom, joy and mercy. For a lack of better words, **each day matters**.

If time stopped in an instant, be it weather or war, would you be able to know that your life mattered for Christ?

Answer this honestly: _____ YES _____ NO

List some of the things that you think might get in the way of living the life Christ intended for you to live (barriers):

Barriers   **Bridges**

_____ ~_____

_____ ~_____

Now go back, by each item listed and write what you think you could do to overcome this obstacle (bridges). If you do not know, then write a prayer on that line for God to guide you. In life there are many barriers, so this can be equally true in our Christian walk. No matter what is going on around us, if we could bring our attention to how it is "with our soul" we would find a need to seek bridges to cross those barriers in order to be in full relationship with God. This becomes not just important to us, but to those we encounter.

Many times we forget our walk doesn't just matter to us—it also matters to someone else. John 15:16-17 says, "You did not choose Me, but I chose you and appointed you that you should go and bear fruit, and that your fruit should remain, that whatever you ask the Father in My name He may give you. These things I command you, that you love one another."

Turn in your Bible and write the translation reference (KJV/NKJV/NIV/ The Message/etc.) and the scripture of John 15:16 below (you will be asked to write this next week as well):

_____

_____

_____

Let this passage sink into your very soul. God chose you! And in doing so, He has appointed you. He has called all of us to bear the fruit He has planted in us. Take a moment and read the whole beginning of John 15. I am not going to spend time in it today; however consider this. Maybe you grew up in church and just have always had that relationship with God and cannot pin down a conversion experience, but you know in your heart you belong to God: heart and soul. Maybe you do not have a story at all just yet. That is okay any way you look at it because He is God. Or maybe you do! In reality, we all have some story, somewhere of who Jesus is to us and why we love Him so.

Regardless of how you identify with the concept of having a story, I believe God has a plan to use each of us if we will allow Him to. Verse sixteen (16), of John 15, is my life verse because it reminds me Whose I am. Immanuel, God with us, means not only did He choose us, but He resides in us. We were chosen by Him and when we accept that, He will abide in us. That is why we do not have to be concerned with 'the how' He can use us, but instead 'the how' we will let Him use us. We have to be deliberate and set aside time for Him daily, seeking His will in our lives. Someone was deliberate in inviting you to church, or showing you Christ's love. You too should be that deliberate.

I asked you to look at John 15:16, because in being deliberate, we need to understand more of what that might imply. We have a responsibility to bear the fruit He has planted in us, so that someone else can "remember". So as you end this week's assignment, I challenge you to ensure your walk with Him is deliberate.

Before wrapping up, let's look at what it might mean to "bear fruit." To do this, let's look to one of the twelve letters that Paul wrote to the early churches. Bearing fruit is not "how much you do," but instead "how you do it!" In Galatians Paul identifies that by not getting caught up on legalisms of how to serve Christ, we should instead be exhibiting characteristics of Christ in order to walk in the Spirit. At the time he wrote this letter, it is believed that the Galatians were exhibiting extreme legalistic views on one hand, while on the other they were completely lawless. So in this letter to the Galatians, Paul addresses that the freedom in Christ is the freedom found in loving one another and doing the right thing.

Let's look further at the term "fruit." In Galatians, chapter 5:16-26, we are instructed to walk in the Spirit so that we will not walk in flesh. Even though in our world today, time is an issue, when we keep ourselves rooted in God and not the hustle and bustle of the world, the fruit we can produce will keep us from walking in the flesh, and instead exemplify our walk in the Spirit. Read Galatians 5:22-23 and list the nine fruits of the spirit:

_____, _____, _____, _____, _____, _____,

_____, _____ and _____ _____.

Now look back at those fruits and circle any that you feel you need to work more on. Place a heart around those you feel like you do well, or that which others have commented on your doing before. Notice that "Kindness" is one of those fruits.   Read the quotes listed below and choose two to summarize what they mean to you:

Kindness is the language which the deaf can hear and the blind can see.
Mark Twain
MEANS: _____
_____

"People are often unreasonable and self-centered. Forgive them anyway.
If you are kind, people may accuse you of ulterior motives. Be kind anyway.
If you are honest, people may cheat you. Be honest anyway.
If you find happiness, people may be jealous. Be happy anyway.
The good you do today may be forgotten tomorrow. Do good anyway.
Give the world the best you have and it may never be enough. Give your best anyway.
For you see, in the end, it is between you and God. It was never between you and them anyway."
Kent M. Keith
MEANS: _____
_____

"For attractive lips, speak words of kindness.
For lovely eyes, seek out the good in people.
For a slim figure, share your food with the hungry.
For beautiful hair, let a child run their fingers through it once a day.
For poise, walk with the knowledge that you never walk alone.
People, more than things, have to be restored, renewed, revived, reclaimed, and redeemed. Remember, if you ever need a helping hand, you will find one at the end of each of your arms.
As you grow older, you will discover that you have two hands, one for helping yourself and the other for helping others."
Sam Levinson
MEANS: _____
_____

"I hope you will have a wonderful year, that you'll dream dangerously and outrageously, that you'll make something that didn't exist before you made it, that you will be loved and that you will be liked, and that you will have people to love and to like in return. And, most importantly (because I think there should be more kindness and more wisdom in the world right now), that you will, when you need to be, be wise, and that you will always be kind."
Neil Gaiman
MEANS: _____

"You cannot do a kindness too soon, for you never know how soon it will be too late."
Ralph Waldo Emerson
MEANS: _____
_____

"Few will have the greatness to bend history itself, but each of us can work to change a small portion of events. It is from numberless diverse acts of courage and belief that human history is shaped. Each time a man stands up for an ideal, or acts to improve the lot of others, or strikes out against injustice, he sends forth a tiny ripple of hope, and crossing each other from a million different centers of energy and daring those ripples build a current which can sweep down the mightiest walls of oppression and resistance."
Robert F. Kennedy
MEANS: _____
_____

"Nothing is so much calculated to lead people to forsake sin as to take them by the hand and to watch over them in tenderness. When persons manifest the least kindness and love to me, O what pow'r it has over my mind."
Joseph Smith Jr.
MEANS: _____
_____

"The words of the tongue should have three gatekeepers: Is it true? Is it kind? Is it necessary?"
Arabian proverb
MEANS: _____
_____

Now, look to Titus in the Bible. What was the ultimate act of kindness identified in Titus 3:4?
_____
_____

Christ giving Himself on the cross to save us from our sins was the ultimate price for one to pay, and scripture identifies it in this verse as an act of kindness. Wow! What a strong word. Kindness seems kind of like a passive word, a gentle act. But reading it in this context, it is so unbelievably powerful.

'Kindness,' in some scripture, is from the Greek word, "chrestos," which means a matter of the heart, goodness towards others as found in Galatians 5:22. This translation tends to lean more favorably to the common English usage of the word today. However, the word can also come from "philanthropia" as translated in Titus, where it is the Greek word meaning God's love for us, "His love towards man[2]." This makes the simple word, "kindness," take on a whole new meaning, doesn't it?

Do we really strive to be Christ-like in all we say and do? This word is important to understand because it is the act of representation—the way we live our life as a witness to Christ. Just like someone bore their fruit for us, once upon a time, we too need to do that for others. Kindness is one of the fruits we are called to bear and one that I attribute so many of the Godly examples in my life to. So, can you think of at least one person who represented "chrestos" or "philanthropia" in your life? If so, list them below and describe why:

_____

_____

---

[2] Vine's Complete Expository Dictionary of Old & New Testament Words, Unger & White, 1996, p 343

If you read Chapters 1-5 from <u>A Teacher's Prayer</u>, what were some examples of kindness in those chapters? List two specific examples.

1._____

_____

2. _____

_____

When taking time to write this study, I am prayerful that you are aware that God really does use you daily. I am hopeful that the words you read in scripture become more powerful and enlightening than ever before and that we who know Immanuel, going forward do not take words like "kindness" lightly anymore. It is a fruit we are to bear and that is one of the many ways we do represent God daily. There is so much God can reveal to you and I pray that you will seek this whole heartedly.

In closing, revisit Psalms 90:12 "Teach us to number our days that we may gain a heart of wisdom." Write a devotional prayer to the Lord with specific requests for a recommitment and/or remembrance in your life. Remember how you came to know the Lord, how excited you were to grow in Him and share Him with others around you and commit to refreshing yourself today.

_____

_____

_____

_____

_____

_____

_____

Isaiah 33:6: *Wisdom and knowledge will be the stability of your times, and the strength of salvation; The fear of the Lord is His treasure.*

Date:_____

NOTES /JOURNAL

Session II~CHOICES

Prayer Line for whom this week:

Times set aside for God this week:

Total Time	Date & Day

Who needs a note this week?

Name	Address

Scripture for the week: John 15:16

Session II ~ CHOICES

Reading

A Teacher's Prayer – Chapters 6~9
Bible Passages outlined in Assignment for Reflection

Class Segment

Choices are handed to us every second. Whether or not to be here is a choice. Whether or not to do your assignment is a choice. But how do we make our choices? We need to really drive home that choices are OURS to make. Consider the following scenario then select the option most likely to be your response. Even though the circumstances might not apply to you, part-time job, kids, etc.—work with me here for a moment and pretend. Put yourself in the situation and try to respond with the first thing that comes to mind. It is, after all, just an exercise.

You are running late for work one morning because your child was not yet ready for school. After calling up the stairs every few minutes with the time left remaining: 5 minutes…1 minute, now 3 minutes late and so on, Janie finally comes running down the stairs, apologizing and explaining that she couldn't find her shoes, only to find you waiting at the last step with a frustrated look.

"I'm sorry," Janie states, a little put out for your impatience, but knowing to be careful with what she says to you.

You whirl around the corner, headed toward the kitchen counter to grab your coffee and bag. Turning around you realize you have lost your daughter again.

"Janie, where are you? It's late!" you call out in a raised tone.

"I have to grab my books," she states more soft spoken than before, emerging from the living room. Dragging her bag on the floor while trying to zip it and make her way towards the door, she moves quicker. The uh-oh expression on her face shows you, Janie knows you are not happy.

Walking hurriedly outside, you push the unlock button on the remote as Janie is running ahead of you to get into the car, not to give you any more reason to fuss. Jumping in the car, you quickly place your coffee in the holder, close the door, pull your seatbelt across your chest while starting the ignition, put the car in reverse and then begin to back up out of your driveway, as you do routinely every day. At that exact moment you decide to look into your rearview mirror, and simultaneously feel and hear, *bump*. Immediately hitting the brakes,

"Crud!" you exclaim. In a whispered tone to Janie, while looking at her in disbelief, you state, "I forgot he is home."

Knowing that your son is sleeping in, because he's on break from college, you put the car in park and get out, dreading the outcome. All of a sudden running late is not important anymore.

Choose your most "honest" likely response:

____ I am such a goof. I can't believe I didn't look in the mirror. (Get out of the car laughing but dreading the damage you might have caused.)

____ If Janie hadn't been running late, I wouldn't have been so stressed out and would've paid attention to my surroundings instead of being in such a hurry backing out.

_____ Why in the world did he park right there, when there is another spot in the driveway? How in the world would I have known his car was there? There should have been no reason to look in my rearview mirror in my own driveway!
_____ All of the above

You can see in this example how many choices can be made. Most importantly, how one can react to a situation. Maybe you can actually relate to this, or maybe not. Before we discuss, let's do one more scenario.

You have the pleasure of being able to work a part-time job that allows you to be off in time to pick your child up from school. It is the last day of the month, and your job has to be completed before you leave for the end of the day, no matter how long it takes. Plus there is no way you can run late due to the dentist appointment that follows school on this particular day.

That morning, work is going along smoothly and as afternoon approaches, you are designated to run out and grab pizza for everyone at a drive thru. You agree, knowing that it will be quick. You agree also knowing that the mail hasn't run yet and you are unable to post the final checks until it gets there. Besides the morning has been smooth for the end of the month, which is usually comparable to a "It's a Monday" syndrome. Since it should be there by the time you get back, you head towards the door. As luck would have it, you got caught up on the phone with a customer and therefore it is nearing about a quarter until one o'clock by the time you leave, only to see the mail lady pulling in. Knowing it is not that long before three fifteen arrives, you are no longer at ease and know this must be a quick run.

You get in your car and drive to the restaurant. Going through the line, you ask for the orders. The guy at the window takes your money and asks you to pull forward; stating it will be just a minute, because they just sold out and they are making more. You say, "Thank you," and move up.

While waiting, you take the opportunity to call your spouse and check in on his or her day. As you are speaking, you realize you have been able to talk way too long. Several cars have come and gone, through the drive-thru, while you have been sitting there. Looking down to see it is now after one o'clock, your voice begins escalating, as you talk to your spouse about how you can't believe it is taking this long. Realizing how aggravating you are getting, hang up the phone and walk into the restaurant.

"Excuse me?!" you demand of the guy behind the counter, as you walk in. He is in the back, near the oven and he can't hear you.
You must say it louder to get his attention, and suddenly realize the young man that took your order at the drive-thru window is in the back laughing and cutting up with another guy, tossing a towel around. "EXCUSE ME!" you demand.
Recognizing you, he stops in his tracks, walks up to you with his oddest expression and begins to apologize, because he admits, "I am so sorry, I forgot your order."

Choose from the following:
_____ You are ticked, there is no excuse for forgetting an order! He shouldn't be working in fast foods, obviously. You have a limited amount of time to get back to finish your work so that you can stay on schedule. No excuses.
_____ You laugh it off and realize it is no big deal. He obviously knows he messed up. Then you think "he better give me my food for free".
_____ You are upset but realize everyone makes a mistake and that is all this was.

This scenario actually happened to me, and the first response was my immediate reaction. Let me tell you though, that God worked on me in that moment. I had been doing a Bible study and was therefore reading my Bible each day and praying. I think because of that, I became convicted. When I walked into that restaurant, my first response was aggravation; however as soon as I saw the look on his face, I was convicted, *Haven't you ever made a mistake before? How are you representing Me?* "Oh!" is all I can say. I know there is a difference in how I relate to people and situations around me, when I am actively spending time with God. I am pleased to report, my frustration turned to joy, and I told the waiter, "No problem, we all make mistakes." He quickly got my order ready and threw in free sauce for the trouble.

In both of these scenarios, completely different except my stress level I guess, you should realize that placing blame on others never solves anything or makes us any happier. In the car in the first scenario, that was me too, and my reaction to that one was to laugh at myself. Thank goodness Anthony (my son) could laugh also. I just know that in the whole scheme of life, we have stresses that come upon us, and people are watching how we handle those stresses. When we stay in God, we humbly respond to things differently. This week's lesson will be about being aware of your ins and outs of your daily life and focusing on how you represent Christ.

Assignment of Reflection

If you haven't yet, be sure to fill in your list to start this week, then pray before continuing. Remember that in last week's assignment we would revisit the verse around John 15:16, "He chose you and appointed you…" but let's begin in another area of scripture first. "To choose" is a verb that is used in the Old Testament 170 times[3]. God started choosing men, with Abram, and the Old Testament is filled with examples of God loving His people to the point, that He "chose" them. We could even argue He chose Adam, since He created him. This week's assignment will focus on God choosing people…what does the beginning of Deuteronomy 4:37 say?

"And because He loved your fathers, therefore He _____ their descendants after them;…"

In Deut 7:7-8, "His choice" also led to the redemption of His people from Egypt. Over and over, one can find examples of "choice" in the Bible. Looking to the New Testament, choice was also associated with calling people. What happened in Luke 6:13?

_____

_____

Note here that Christ called his "disciples" to Him and from them, He chose twelve apostles. Keep this tucked away for we will study this a bit more in the lessons to come; however today we will focus on the fact that He chose.

On the top of the next page, draw a line from the passage to the verse it belongs to:

---

[3] Vine's Complete Expository Dictionary of Old & New Testament Words, Unger & White, 1996, p 35

John 15:16   "Just as He chose us in Him before the foundation of the world, that we should be holy and without blame before Him in love..."

Eph. 1:4   "You did not choose Me, but I chose you and appointed you that you should go and bear fruit, and that your fruit should remain, that whatever you ask..."

Last week opened by talking about how and why we came to know the Lord. Now let's begin internalizing how we represent Him. To get to the nitty-gritties of that, it is important to understand and accept that He chose us and uses us daily, or at least He wants to. Go back to the answer you just selected for John 15:16 and circle it and pray over it. Let it really sink in that God chose you. He did! So, what are you going to do with that knowledge? In the book, A Teacher's Prayer, I spoke about how God used different people like, Tiffany, Tom and Grandma to be His light to me. They had to make choices on how they related to me and how to help me. I believe those opportunities are around us daily.

In this week's reading of Chapters 6-10, you will see the odds continue to stack against me, Tammy. I made choices, and continuously other people did also, which provided enough guidance and hope to make it through some really tough situations. When I first sat down to write A Teacher's Prayer, I was telling my story. Over time though, I became convicted that it wasn't my story, but God's and how He used people to help me along the way. I then spent time editing and retelling the story from the perspective that everyone does make a difference, negative or positive, and that we can choose how we want to be remembered. This devotional is to challenge you to choose how you can represent Christ. Just like the scenarios discussed in the Class Segment, everything we do daily (even the simple normal day to day routines of our lives) can and does, reflect Christ to those around us. And when we are grounded in Christ, we simply respond differently to things.

Do you believe God chose you? ___YES ___NO

Why or Why not?_____

_____

Do you think your relationship with Christ reflects how you respond to people and situations? Please explain:

_____

_____

_____

With that in mind, let's consider tough times in life. Tough times are just like choices, usually there are at least two options. In the end, it is what we do with those options. Tough times can make us or break us, just like our choices. There will be times when other people make bad choices, and those choices affect us through no fault of our own, simply situational. Then there are those times when the effects are consequences of our own choices. Regardless, if we learn to look to God for strength and understanding, we will find He can work His glory through it all. That includes us being available to be used of Him in tough times. Immanuel, God is with us, should also mean to us that God goes with us—no matter what and no matter who.

You may say, "I already understand this concept, so what is the point of revisiting it?" If so, look at it through your actual reactions to tough choices in your life or those around you?

Are you currently going through a tough time that you need confidence of God's presence in? _____YES _____NO

I am only asking you to answer, not to identify in writing at this time. What about observing another friend who is going through a tough time? Do they need to feel God's presence through you? _____YES _____NO

Where do you find the strength to make the choices and responses to situations around you, be it for yourself or for others?

_____

_____

Open your scripture to Ephesians 3:14-21: *"For this reason I **bow** my knees to the Father of our Lord Jesus Christ, from whom the whole family in heaven and earth is named, that he would grant you, according to the riches of His glory, to be strengthened with might through His Spirit in the inner man, that Christ may dwell in your hearts through faith; that you being **rooted** and **grounded** in love, may be able to **comprehend** with all the saints what is the width and length and depth and height to know the love of Christ which passes knowledge; that you may be filled with all the fullness of God."*

Our strength comes from *His Spirit in the inner man.* His Spirit here in Greek is pneuma, meaning, "the wind (to breathe), invisible, immaterial and powerful[4]" which denotes in this verse the Spirit of the Glory of God. According to this scripture, God's glory is within us, His Spirit, which enables Christ to dwell in our hearts. Immanuel—God with us? Absolutely! God is with us when we are willing to be rooted and grounded in Him! And when we really grasp this meaning we will see our responses to many choices will be differently handled in a good way.

This passage goes on to tell us that if we are rooted and grounded in love, then we do not have to make sense of the why's of this world. Our earthly minds want to know all the answers but all we really need is to be filled with the fullness of God because His love surpasses all understanding. So don't get caught up on the whys, but instead learn to trust Him and be filled with Him. My prayer for you is to have a new appreciation for, and understanding of, 'Immanuel.' So where can you start?

_____

_____

I use my Bible study time to draw closer to God, along with prayer, in order to try and stay in His will. What do you do to actively draw closer to God?

_____

_____

---

[4] Vine's Complete Expository Dictionary of Old & New Testament Words, Unger & White, 1996, pp 593-594

Continuously putting effort into drawing closer to God will help us to live a more Christ-like life to all we encounter, even allowing us to forgive those we know not how to, on our own.

List examples of renewal that you saw in Chapters 6-10 from A Teacher's Prayer, or anything that particularly spoke to you in the reading.

_____

_____

_____

_____

When I draw closer to God in prayer and in studying His word, I can find a peace that passes all understanding. The very peace, which helped me to respond differently in the second scenario with the pizza order. The peace that helped me make it through, and still does, some very big trials in my life. May you be filled with the fullness of God; *pleroma, that which is a thing full; it is thus used of the grace and truth manifested in Christ, including all of His virtues and excellencies; the completeness of His being.*

Please let this sink in. We need to come to a place spiritually, that we do not repay evil for evil, and that we know that the grace and truth only found through the manifestation of Christ, gives us true fulfillment in life, and we are thereby enabled to all of His virtues and excellencies. Now how excellent is that? What do you need to do to respond to this closing or who do you need to bow down in prayer for? Commit to it as we close this day.

Dear God, fill me, _____(your name), with pleroma, with

mercy and truth that I, _____(your name) may abound in

true fulfillment of You when dealing with _____ (any issues or personalities you are currently in conflict with or the name of a friend you need to stand in the gap for)

dear God! Amen! Help me to remember, God, that everything I do to anyone else, I do to you.

May you walk with me, _____ (your name), and guide me to be more

pleasing to You! AMEN!

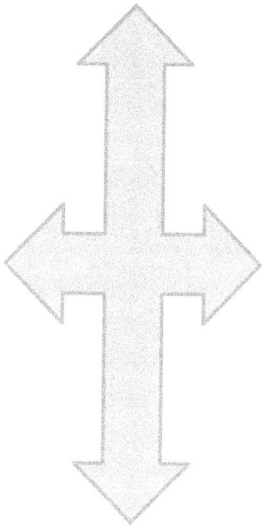

Date:_____

NOTES /JOURNAL

Session III~RENEW

Prayer Line for whom this week:

Times set aside for God this week:

Total Time	Date & Day

Who needs a note this week?

Name	Address

Scripture for the week: 2 Cor 5:17

SESSION III ~ RENEW

Reading
A Teacher's Prayer – Chapters 10-13
Bible Passages outlined in Assignment for Reflection

Class Segment
What does the word create mean to you? What about when we talk about God? God is the Creator. Not just of all that is life, He is Creator of all that is good, all that is, but for what purpose? He did not just create us and walk away as if we were some opaque image he conjured up in a passing thought. He created us in His own image. Turn to Gen 1:1, 27, 31 and: Fill in the following: 1 *God created the _____ and the _____. 27 So God created man in _____ own _____, in the image of God He created him; male and female He created them. 31 Then God saw everything that He had made and indeed it was very _____.* (NKJV)

Also turn to Ephesians 2:4-10. Make sure to read each line slowly and clearly, to allow the words to really become embedded into your heart and understanding. Now write down your understanding of Ephesians 2:10:

_____

_____

_____

This week's lesson will begin by acknowledging it is by the grace and mercy of the great Creator that we are alive in Christ and that it is our faith, not our works, which warrant us a personal walk with Him.

Assignment for Reflection
Let's begin by spending a few moments of quiet time with God, focusing on Psalms 51:10. Please write the verse below:

_____

_____

_____

Turn to Genesis 1:1 and list the common word used in the passage above and in the very first scripture of God's Holy Word _____. Turn also to 2 Corinthians 5:17 and fill in the following: *Therefore, if anyone is in Christ, he is a new _____; old things have _____ _____; behold, all things have become _____.*

Creation in these passages represents a request for a radical cleansing that only God can provide. To create the universe, to create a clean heart in us, both are the same uses of the definition of the word *ktisis*,[5] which is the creative act of God. In 2 Corinthians the reference is what man is in Christ, the consequence of becoming anew through the creative act of God.

Looking back to Genesis, *bara*[6] expresses God's act in creating something out of nothing. In Psalms, *bara* implies God bringing something into existence out of nothing. That is the God we serve, making something out of nothing. Can you find evidence of where God has done this in your life? _____

_____

_____

Take a moment and give a prayer of Thanksgiving for the way you have already seen God at work in your life; then ask Him to open your heart, mind and soul as you continue through this devotion.

Not long ago my family visited Orlando, Florida. At Universal Studios and Islands of Adventure, we had the opportunity to experience remarkable and magnificent creations with technology, making for realistic holograms, amazing 3D and 4D shows and ridiculously crazy roller coasters with extra appeal. I was in awe of the reality of all the props and technicalities that go into movies can actually play out in real life adventure, even if only for brief moments in time. I then began thinking about how skilled some of those engineers and stage hands are, to work together to create such a pleasurable experience. I would not be sharing this at all without admitting I am good NOT experiencing the Hulk roller coaster again (which was my favorite). We rushed through all of the thrill rides and enjoyed them, but one time was enough for me and well worth it for my children to experience.

To wrap up our short lived-vacation we took the last half day of our trip and drove to the ocean. For me, visiting the ocean was the climax of the trip. I have always found inspiration there with the sounds of the waves crashing against the rocks. How majestic that was and still is for me. Words can't even begin to express the sheer peace and awe that mesmerized me for the umpteenth time, as I looked out. I always reminisce back to the first time I saw the ocean, with my youth group at age sixteen. I could not fathom the great vastness my eyes would behold. And yet the same feeling still overcomes me to this day. W*ow,* I thought, *God created this for me to enjoy? He made something this enormous and is able to contain it within the gravity of our planet? How astounding and marvelous is that?* Really think about that for a moment with me. It still simply amazes me how technologically-advanced and mind-blowing our God is with each new discovery. He creates such wonderful intricately run things like the

[5] Vine's Complete Expository Dictionary of Old & New Testament Words, Unger & White, 1996, p 137
[6] Vine's Complete Expository Dictionary of Old & New Testament Words, Unger & White, 1996, p 51

oceans. I hope you slow down and look around to appreciate all of the creations He has provided for you.

Seasons changing make it easy to understand this type of creation appreciation. Spring usually brings a time of renewal with all of the rains replenishing our grounds. What about the fruit trees, producing luscious and succulent flavors, for our pure enjoyment which, I remind you, started out as simple flower blooms? Summer brings gorgeous green hues on trees and leaves, flowers brilliantly covering lawns and roadsides to enhance eye appeal for what purpose? Joy? Or maybe just to provide shade from the sun? What about the Technicolor of fall and the leaves fully clothing their trees with an array of a true artist's palette of oranges, reds, and yellows. Even when they fall, can't you just imagine the smiles on our faces when we get to enjoy children piling up a mountain of leaves only to jump into them with the sheer excitement of watching them not only cushion their fall, but scatter again. And in winter, if the amazing pure white snow that first falls tickles your senses for a hot cup of cocoa or a crackling fire, then that works too. Of course I could've chosen some negative thoughts, but that's just it. My choice and I choose joy.

For Pete's sake, we could discuss the amazingness of the body healing, the birth of any newborn baby and the magnificence of the various animals covering our earth and in the waters, or whatever else you can think of. And that is what I hope for confidence in that you to take from this day; the reminder that just as amazing as all of those creations are to you, so you are to God. He created you and what He creates is good—it is very good. Good on God's level—well, that's about as good as it gets—wouldn't you say?

Stop for a moment and think about Creation then share below an example or two of how God has 'wowed' you in His creation. Be prepared to share this with the class. (Don't worry, you do not have to provide graphic descriptions, simple statements are just as powerful too.)

_____

_____

_____

_____

_____

Thank you for taking time to reflect on how God's creation has wowed you. I want to emphasize again, that He, our God, holds that same 'wow factor' which we hold over His creation, over you! Now open to Genesis 1:26 – 31. What did God create on the sixth day? _____ In whose image? _____ In verse 31, what did God say about what He had made? It was very _____.

Now look at Isaiah 40: 27-31 and paraphrase what this passage says to you.

_____

_____

_____

In the passage of Isaiah 40:27-31 the reference of God's people is of Israel and Jacob who felt that God had forgotten them. Their concept of God was not large enough to realize there was no need to be discouraged—they needed to be reminded He was and is the great Creator. When we remember to Who we give service, His power is so big that our insufficiencies are not challenges, at least not for Him; even though they might seem to us. So what I hope you take from this is that when we remember **Who** we serve, what do we know? Turn to Matthew 19:26 and fill in the following: *But Jesus looked at them and said to them, "with men this is _____, but with God all things are _____.*

Is there anything that seems impossible to you lately? What about anything in your life that has been hindering your walk with Christ, specifically in your calling or maybe even your relationship with Him?_____

_____

If so, remember think about how to go about renewing yourself? It is always good to take time to renew ourselves in any aspect. It may be education to continue improving skills in a changing world. It may be a water break during exercise so as not to dehydrate. We need that in our walk with God too, so that we are reflective of Him in our lives and not of ourselves. Notice back in Isaiah 40:29-31 that Creator God, the awesome power of God, gives us the opportunity to renew or to exchange our weakness if we seek Him and wait. Take a moment and pray over what you wrote in the space above, asking God to renew your spirit and believe in the possibility of peace and resolution.

Now, revisit Psalms 51:10 and please take time to re-read it before proceeding. David calls out to God to create in him a new heart, but not only that, he asks Him to renew his spirit. When we accepted Christ, we too asked him to make us new in Him. More times than not, we journey with excitement finding ways to grow closer to God by Bible Study and service to His call on our lives, just like we talked about in Session I. Here's the thing I think we may forget at times: God knows our heart and that we love Him and want to serve Him; and likewise He is aware that at times, we overdo it. Maybe by providing us with David's insight in His holy word, God can remind us that He understands there are times our spirits need to be renewed. This is true whether you reach a burnout level or you simply want God to open even more doors for you. When we give so much time to our family, our work and our church or other areas, we can easily tire especially when we do not find a time to renew ourselves. Likewise our spiritual lives need renewal—just as David's did. I believe God is honored when we remember that we need Him to renew us, and that we cannot do it on our own.

Match up some of the examples found in scripture that we demonstrate a need to commit to renewal in our lives and in our spirits.

Col 3:10   *...and be renewed in the spirit of your mind, and that you put on the new man which was created according to God, in true righteousness and holiness.*

Eph 4:23-24   *...renewed in knowledge according to the image of Him who created him...*

2 Cor 4:16   *...not by works of righteousness which we have done, but according to His mercy he saves us, through the washing of regeneration and renewing of the Holy Spirit,...*

Titus 3:5   *Therefore we do not lose heart...yet the inward man is being renewed day by day.*

If any of the above scriptures speak to you directly, circle them then pray them to God asking for the renewal. In closing, you will see often times the scripture immediately surrounding the word renew is proceeded or succeeded with the word create somewhere close by. The word create by definition is the process of developing, generating, building or shaping an idea to a current concrete form or action. So when you ask God to create a new heart in you, you are asking him to continue through the process of developing you and in doing so renewing you.

Now take time to list some ways that you have found spiritual renewal in the past:

_____   _____

_____   _____

Beside those listed, place a check to the right of the ones you see ongoing actively in your life right now. Circle the ones you know you need to put more focus on. Now take a moment and pray that God will allow you to renew in the ways listed above and in ways even unknown to you at this time.

Remember God uses us where we are and provides us with what we need to accomplish His will if we seek Him. If something is consuming your heart, or getting in the way of your service to Him then realize that spiritual renewal does need to take place, but it cannot just happen by itself. If nothing is consuming, but you are feeling called to do more and just not quite sure what that is, ask Him to reveal it to you.

Now open your scripture to 2 Corinthians 5: 17 again, pray, then fill in the following by substituting your name where directed or filling in scripture where applicable.

Therefore _____(your name)*, if, you, are in Christ,* _____(your name)*, you, are a new creation; old things have*_____ _____*; behold, all things have become* _____*.*

So anything that is old (before this moment in time), that has been hindering any part of life, let it pass away and become new. Know that I am praying for you this whole week long. Each night while you are at home doing your assignment, ask God to open your hearts and minds and remember that Christ does call us to renew our spirits and that is my hope for you this week. If you find yourself in need of renewal in any area of your life or in your church, stop and ask God to create in you a new heart. Ask that He show you how to be able to prioritize what is important and what really does matter to His will in your life. Please use the remaining space to write a prayer, recommitting yourself to anything that has been placed on your heart.

_____

_____

_____

_____

_____

Date:_____

NOTES /JOURNAL

Session IV~Discipleship

Prayer Line for whom this week:

Times set aside for God this week:

Total Time	Date & Day

Who needs a note this week?

Name	Address

Scripture for the week: Matthew 28:19~20

SESSION IV ~ DISCIPLESHIP

Reading
A Teacher's Prayer – Chapters 14 - Epilogue
Bible Passages outlined in Assignment for Reflection

Class Segment
Here's a new thought for you, that I hope will begin to bring this devotional study of self-reflection full circle. What does Disciple mean to you? _____

_____

Circle the words you think mean disciple: Messenger   Envoy   Ambassador   You

Have you ever thought of yourself as a disciple? YES__ NO __

Pulling translations from the Holman Bible Dictionary, let's review the word, "disciple[7]". An English word known as apostle, it originates from the Greek word 'apostolos' and means ambassador, messenger or envoy. This word is closely associated with the verb 'to send,' and refers to one who is sent on behalf of another. In the Old Testament, the Hebrew verb for sending was 'shalach' and is translated as 'apostello' in the Greek Old Testament, the Septuagint, it means divine spokesmen or apostles. Using this paragraph, complete the following:

'Apostolos" means ambassador, _____ or envoy and is closely related to the verb _____, which refers to one who is sent on behalf of _____.

God desires to make each of us fishers of men, messengers, or disciples. A call to the early Christians and one that still holds true today is that He wants to send us out to spread His message of love to others. The method that He chooses for us to use will vary by each individual and each situation, with different talents and needs. Be praying that God will reveal to you a restful spirit as you work on this week's assignment.

Assignment for Reflection
Historically, God called His people to reach out as ambassadors for Him. We see this in stories dispersed throughout the Old Testament. Can you write down two or three people that immediately come to mind from OT as ambassadors of God?

_____   _____   _____

Looking at New Testament and the translations covered in this assignment, the idea of someone sent on behalf of another in the Old Testament is certainly in line with the same ideas of the

---

[7] Holman Bible Dictionary, 1991, Holman Bible Publishers, pp. 362-364

term apostle in the New Testament. Many scholars hold to the belief that the word apostle in the New Testament is reserved for those who held eye witness accounts to the ministry of Jesus Christ as well as the resurrected Lord.

Now consider the word disciple translated to English from the Latin root, 'didaskalos.' Its meaning is that of learner or pupil and describes "one who follows one teaching[8]".

Disciples' primary functions were to pass along the studies and learned speeches and knowledge of their teacher. "In rabbinic Judaism the term 'disciple' referred to the one who was committed to the interpretations of Scripture and religious tradition given him by the master or rabbi.[9]" Pay close attention to this next part: these traditions were learned by meetings that allowed question and answer time, instructions, memorization and repetition, with an uncanny devotion to absorb and pass on the teachings of the master. Is any of this sounding familiar to you? Why do you gather in small group studies or Sunday School classes or Sunday services at church? Remember, for you, what is at the heart of your gathering time and then take time to list it below:

_____   _____

_____   _____

Understanding just how relevant the word disciple is can be measured by how many times it is found in the New Testament: 233 times in the Gospels and 28 times in Acts. While customarily and routinely this word refers to followers of Jesus Christ, there are examples of other uses of this word. Match up the scripture to the disciples' reference below:

Luke 11:1	Pharisees
John 9:28	Moses
Matthew 22:16	John

Notice all of the different types of disciples being referenced. We tend to lean towards the story of Jesus and His twelve disciples. Again the word 'disciple' is representative of those who followed a teacher and his instructions and were willing to pass them on. However, our focus will be on Christ. Do you consider yourself a disciple of Christ? Look back to your answer in the Class Segment. Now turn in your Bible to the Great Commission found in Matthew 28: 16-20, and complete v. 19-20 below.

"Go therefore, and make _____ of all the _____, baptizing them in the name of the Father and of the Son and of the Holy Spirit, teaching them to observe all things that I have _____ you; and lo, I am with you always, even to the end of the age. Amen."

---

[8] Holman Bible Dictionary, 1991, Holman Bible Publishers, pp. 362-364
[9] Holman Bible Dictionary, 1991, Holman Bible Publishers, p.364

"After Christ's resurrection He appeared to the eleven disciples in Galilee on the mountain. He appointed them (16) and when they saw Him, they began to worship Him, but still some doubted (17)." In the remaining verses (18-20) Jesus affirms His authority over heaven and earth and commissions His disciples to go and make more disciples of all nations in the name of the Father, Son, and the Holy Spirit, teaching and reminding them that He would be with them always. Christ commissioned his disciples to go and make disciples of many nations. What does your Bible state as the adjective accompanying the limitations of nations? _____ The NKJV states, "all nations..."

You do after all, gather in meetings to learn the teachings and interpretations of religious beliefs to live your life as an example of being "new in Christ." _____YES ـ____NO

Before asking you to revisit the thoughts on "why you?", I want to share a scripture that I have read over many times, but about a year ago it took on new specific meaning and direction in my life. It reassigned a responsibility I had forgotten. Revelation 12:11 reads, "And they overcame him ('the accuser') by the blood of the Lamb and by the word of their testimony."

For me, small group Bible studies have allowed an opportunity for fellow brothers and sisters in Christ to come together and share the struggles and praises they have experienced in their own lives. By discussing and sharing through Christian fellowship and by searching scripture for wisdom on God's plans for their lives, time and again I have witnessed others being able to overcome quite daunting circumstances. And I have witnessed amazing acts of goodness as well. We have already covered some examples in the book, but also there are the teachers who threw me a surprise Christmas and Mama Flo and Sharon Spann and Mr. Cunningham and of course Ms. Lokey and the countless others who followed God's lead to intercede in some way in my life. They were people who lived their lives in accordance with their religious teachings and beliefs. Their examples have stayed with me and for that I am incredibly grateful.

The phrase "it takes a village to raise a child," couldn't be truer than what I experienced. So many people impacted my life and because of it, my life is different. That is one of the things that the church is. It is the village, in the community, with people gathering to learn about exemplifying and carrying out Christ' love, that this concept came alive. It was in the church that I received a solid foundation through stories from scripture and music. There have been many times when a particular scripture, story or hymn that I learned in church brought me hope or joy in the midst of uncertain circumstances and sometimes desperate time; because those songs, those hymns remind me that I am loved. I believe you can say the same. Hopefully, we can agree with what this lesson has said so far, but tell me this, did you know your attendance in gleaning more about God, be it in small group or church or Sunday school, was preparing you to go out? Do you think He means for us to come and receive a message from Him or insight to the life He has called us to and not take it with us when we walk back out those church doors? ____YES ـ____NO

Have you felt God tugging at your heart to step up and lead in a certain area of your church or personal life? If so, list it below:

_____

_____

If not, I ask you to write in the space above, a prayer to God to show you how He can use you. Remember in both instances, if you will pray up and seek His presence, He can do some amazing things through you.

In closing, reflecting back on the translations covered in this assignment, apostle, comes across as a word generally reserved for those with direct eyewitness of the ministry and/or resurrection of the Lord Jesus Christ. Look at John 20:29 and fill in the blanks to a very important message that Christ wanted us to really understand: *Jesus said to him, "Thomas, because you have _____ Me, you have _____. Blessed are those who have not _____ and yet have _____."*

The word disciple became more equivalent to those who believed in and followed Jesus: for all whom, by hearing and believing the faith of Jesus Christ, are called to be disciples. So even though you may not have yet seen Jesus, do you believe? _____ YES _____ NO

Regardless of the title assigned to the follower, the common thread of their meaning was allegiance to Jesus and with that a responsibility to share His teachings. Based on your assignment this week, take a spiritual inventory of the past year in your Bible Study group(s), Sunday School classes and or church time as well as your personal life. Praise God for the ways you've seen Him at work in those areas:

1. _____   5. _____

2. _____   6. _____

3. _____   7. _____

4. _____   8. _____

Next list the challenges you've faced in those areas and that need to be recommitted to the Lord for the upcoming year:

1. _____   3 _____

2. _____   4. _____

Now list two specific successes you've observed or personally experienced in church:

1. _____

2. _____

Conclude this session with a prayer asking God to help you become more aware of opportunities He can use you for, not for works sake, but for the joy of knowing that He has created you, chose you and called you to send forth for His continued sequel!

_____

_____

_____

_____

_____

_____

If you read Chapters 14-Epilogue from A Teacher's Prayer, list any examples of discipleship you saw actively play out.

_____

_____

_____

_____

_____

_____

_____

Date:_____

Notes /Journal

Session V~COURAGE

Prayer Line for whom this week:

Times set aside for God this week:

Total Time	Date & Day

Who needs a note this week?

Name	Address

Scripture for the week: Ephesians 1:4

SESSION V ~ PRAYER

Reading
Bible Passages outlined in Assignment for Reflection

Class Segment
Do you ever find yourself contemplating over things to a point that it becomes just about all you think of? You know: did I do all that I could? Should I really have said that? (Of course not, no-one would ever reflect on that!) I think all of us have, at one time or another, and especially in difficult times, reflected positively and negatively about our decisions, words and actions. Why is this?

_____

_____

Let's face it—at some point in our lives, we all mess up something! Isn't it funny how, when things are royally messed up and we can't seem to work out a solution in our heads that many times we find ourselves on our knees in prayer? We ask God to help us fix it or at least guide us!

So how do we move to not focusing on messing up, but instead focusing on being guided? What might this prayer look like to you? What if we started every day asking Him to guide us and use us? If we prayed this daily, maybe, just maybe, we would worry less about all of the 'what if's,' because our focus would be on Him.

Prayer tends to lead us to an opportunity to trust in something greater, bigger and unexplainable when we cannot make sense of it on our own. Our focus moves from us, where there is no control, to God, where there is hope for control. We are going in this direction because I think it can be easy enough to think of all the ways God could use us, but then we have all the 'what abouts' that get in the way of us trusting fully in Him. Just like any aspect of our life, it is fitting to solidify our concerns through prayer, trusting God to see us through.

A Teacher's Prayer is the title of this book, because it is through prayer so many unexplainable things do occur.

Assignment for Reflection
Let's start today's assignment with contemplation. What does the word **BOW** mean to you? Think of it not just in a Christian text but as an English word.

List all of the uses you can come up with:

Bow: _____

Bow: _____

Bow: _____

Bow: _____

Take those words you just listed and compare to the spiritual word, BOW, as the tilting of our heads or falling prostrate to our knees. Now when I think about going through things in my life, I personally find prayer the most helpful. Trusting in God when nothing else seems to bring solutions or resolutions brings a sense of strength and peace in my life. I also find prayer a necessary element when I am making a major decision in my life: to change jobs, to buy a home or relocate, etc.

Of course when we pray, we can be sitting, standing or the most familiar, bowing. So I posted the word bow (with my thought being that of the bended knee version) on Facebook and asked people to respond to the meaning of the word. No rules, no guidance, I just threw it out there. In turn, these responses got me to pondering how the root word, *bow*, has so many different meanings yet each with relevance to the purpose of this week's lesson. Take a look at some of the different uses and compare as an analogy to the point of this particular lesson.

First look is going to be correlated to the description of the **bow of a ship**. The front of the ship is known as the bow and is where the oarsman can be found. Ponder for a moment, when on our knees we bow, aren't we taking the front stance? Aren't we bowing many times in an effort to stand up against or for something that is weighing in on our hearts, or simply to find direction?

It is on our knees that Christ gives us the power to be in the lead of all situations. There are many stories in the Bible, of godly men and women bowing on their knees for God's guidance. Many times, they are at the front lead of the story on behalf of God.

An example: before Moses led God's people from Egypt, he bowed many times, asking for God's guidance in the road that lay ahead, the road he was chosen to lead God's people on. Can you think of any other example of men or women who bowed in prayer prior to taking the lead on behalf of God? _____

_____

Have you prayed for God to use you to take the lead in something in the past or present?
_____ YES _____NO

I hope, if you haven't yet, you will take a moment and pray for God to make it known to you and trusting Him fully, to lead you.

Let's look at another meaning of the word bow. You've seen them plenty, the **pretty bows tied** into a little girls' hair or onto gifts to spruce up their appearance. Just think if we put that extra touch on each thing in our lives. Maybe not realistic in a time sense, but is there something you maybe should ask God to put that finishing touch on? It may not be a struggle, but a praise. We should always give thanks that God gives us the finishing touches in our lives. Write a prayer thanking God for some finishing touch you have seen in your own life recently.

_____

_____

_____

If you are having trouble finding thanks for something pertaining to you personally, then look around—maybe you have seen Him at work in a friend or family member.

Another direction, maybe you like to hunt (or know someone that does) and thought of a **bow, a tool that is bent of pliable material**. It is used to shoot an arrow with such great force that not only was it a great weapon for hunting, but also for combat. A bow in this sense is proven to work because of mechanical energy. Let's look at the terms and their meanings for just a moment. According to wisegeek.com, Mechanical Energy is made up of the sum of kinetic energy and potential energy.

Kinetic energy has to do with motion and represents the effort required to achieve a current state of velocity from a resting position. Potential energy does not provide anything to change the work or its surroundings, but in its current form, it has the potential to be transformed to kinetic energy. Anytime an object is displaced from its original position, like the string on the bow, and finds that there is energy pulling it back like when released, that is when potential energy tends to exist.

Now why would so much time be spent on this description? Think about what physical activity many of us do when we pray to our Heavenly Father. When we bow on our knees, we too, are either hunting for God's guidance in our lives or trying to combat the things going on around us. Prayer, universally, is communication in general and not just a correspondence for seeking help or counsel from God. Prayer may not include bowing on our knees. We may be driving down the road, walking or sitting.

Use this scale to represent anytime you talk to God. On a scale of 1-7, with 1 being the lowest and 7 being the highest, place a circle on the scale that represents the times you pray as pure conversation with God, just to talk. Place a triangle (for the Trinity who listens, bridges and intervenes) on the scale to represent the times you pray for help or counsel. Place a heart (never ending) on the scale for the representation of the times you simply pray to give thanks to Him.

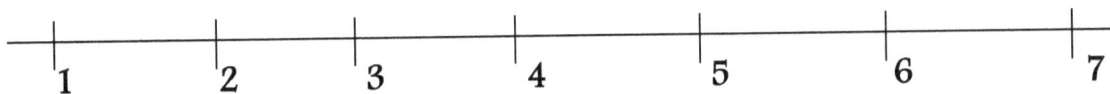

```
 |------|------|------|------|------|------|
 1      2      3      4      5      6      7
```

Do you understand that the kinetic energy of prayer is that we have to put in a certain amount of effort? Please list below how you position yourself when you pray:

_____

_____

Why do we bow? Maybe you bow because you were taught to? Maybe... or maybe you bow when you pray, because you desire a more deliberate effort to achieve a state of peace and contentment or assurance? Or maybe, the only time you bow is when you have absolutely no energy left and are seeking a fulfillment from Him? Sure, this also.

Here's the thing though, just like that bow, we are asking God to shoot our arrow in a direction to conquer. Our kinetic energy may be simply our bowing of knees, but our potential energy comes in being the very same person we knelt down as, yet rising with an assurance of the power of God to transform our situation. Just like the bow helps hunters and warriors to win battles, prayers help us to trust in God and be submissive to His will. Don't miss the submissive part because it is through that submission, we can find peace, direction and strength.

When we know that God is our arrow, or conqueror, we can find the target.

Before we end this devotion assignment, it is relevant that we talk about one more form of **bow, to kneel in humbleness or reverence**. Ephesians is a powerful book written by Paul to the church of Ephesus, believed by many scholars to intentionally circulate throughout other churches too, for teaching and encouragement. Unlike the other letters Paul wrote to address specific problems within the church, the book of Ephesians is believed to proclaim spiritual resources available to Christian believers and to empower the purpose of the church to exalt Christ by drawing on His resources of love, fellowship and maturity in the interactions of spiritual battles.

In Ephesians 1:4, Christ calls us in Him to be _____ and without _____.

Remember last week we discussed how God created us in His image? This means, He also knows how He can use you, but you have to be willing. You have to draw courage to stand up and move forward as He has called you to, and look for ways to serve Him and TRUST Him! Remember, it is on our knees we find the kinetic energy and power of a loving God to sustain and guide us. How will you be guided?

I hope you have had some real one on one time with God to personally reflect on how very much He can and wants to use you. God bless you and may you learn to seek God daily to help you show kindness and courage as His disciple. Remember, "HE CHOSE YOU!"

Use the final page to create a goal of things you would like to see yourself accomplish this upcoming year. How do you intend to grow in God and show God a little more every day? May God go with us in all that we say and do!

Goals:

Dear God, Please help me to commit the following to you this upcoming year:

_____

_____

_____

_____

_____

_____

_____

_____

_____

_____

I Pray, Immanuel!

_____ (signature) / _____ (date)

I hope you have enjoyed this study time and have found the book to represent not my story, but God's story in my life. The message is that we all make a difference in this world and we need to be more deliberate in asking God to use us! God bless-Tammy

Author is available for book signing and speaking engagements, including churches, leadership retreats and conferences, women's groups, high school academic banquets, etc.

For more information please contact ptalbrown@charter.net.

To demonstrate a small example of how much of a difference sharing your testimony can make, be it the way you live your life or even sharing your stories if called to, check out a couple of excerpts of letters/emails received since the publication of A Teacher's Prayer.

SENT VIA EMAIL 12/06/12
SO AMAZING – TONIGHT SEVERAL ELDERS MET ON KNEES AT THE ALTAR TO PRAY FOR THE CHURCH. ONE PRAYER WAS THAT WE WOULD TAKE TAMMY'S WORDS SPOKEN MONDAY TO HEART AND REACH OUT TO THE HURTING. –CHRISTIE, FIRST PRESBYTERIAN CHURCH, SELMA, AL

SENT VIA EMAIL 06/03/12
DEAR MRS. TAMMY,
YOUR BOOK WAS AMAZING! I CRIED TO THINK THAT YOU HAD TO GO THROUGH THAT, IT BREAKS MY HEART TO HEAR OF ANYONE HAVING TO GO THROUGH ANYTHING LIKE YOU DID. WHEN YOU TALKED ABOUT GOING TO VACATION BIBLE SCHOOL, IT GOT ME THINKING ABOUT MYSELF GOING TO VBS AS A KID, THAT IS THE PLACE WHERE I ALSO GOT CLOSER TO GOD AND ACCEPTED HIM INTO MY LIFE. YOUR BOOK WAS VERY TOUCHING, AND I AM GLAD THAT YOU WERE ABLE TO TURN YOUR LIFE AROUND! AS A TEENAGER IT REALLY MAKES ME THINK ABOUT HOW MANY PEOPLE OR POSSIBLY OTHER TEENAGERS THAT I SEE EVERYDAY COULD BE GOING THROUGH THE EXACT SAME THING YOU DID OR SOMETHING CLOSE TO IT. YOUR BOOK HAS MADE ME STEP BACK AND LOOK AT MY LIFE AND HAS HELPED ME MAKE SOME CHANGES TO IT! THE PEOPLE I MAY NOT HAVE ASSOCIATED WITH BEFORE, I TALK TO ON A DAILY BASIS, AND I HAVE EVEN GOTTEN CLOSE TO SOME OF THEM. YOUR BOOK TAUGHT ME THAT EVEN SOMETHING AS SIMPLE AS SAYING "HEY" TO SOMEONE, MAYBE SOMEONE YOU RARELY TALK TO, CAN REALLY MAKE A DIFFERENCE IN THEIR LIFE, AND POSSIBLY BECOME A BLESSING TO YOURS. THANK YOU FOR COMING AND SPEAKING TO SOME OF THE STUDENTS AT MY SCHOOL! WITH CHRISTIAN LOVE,
KALEIGH, STUDENT FROM WINTERBORO HIGH SCHOOL

SENT VIA EMAIL 12/1/12
HI, MRS. TAMMY!
I KNOW I'M VERY LATE AT SENDING THIS EMAIL TO YOU, BUT I WANTED TO SAY HOW MUCH YOU IMPACTED MY LIFE … EVER SINCE I CAME BACK HOME AND BACK TO SCHOOL, I'VE STARTED NOTICING THE LITTLE THINGS ABOUT PEOPLE. HOW THEY ACT OR HOW THEY DRESS, ETC, AND I'VE STARTED TALKING TO THEM. IT'S CRAZY HOW YOU CAN SEE SOMEONE ON A DAILY BASIS, AND NOT HAVE A CLUE AS TO WHAT THEY'RE GOING THROUGH!
I WANTED TO SAY THANK YOU...
SINCERELY,
JACLYN CASTON

YOU CAN ALSO VIEW THE FOX 6 NEWSCAST OUT OF BIRMINGHAM, AL AT:
http://www.myfoxal.com/category/240204/video-landing-page?autoStart=true&topVideoCatNo=default&clipId=7954797#.UKLkBoJZq_8.facebook

Like us on Facebook at: https://www.facebook.com/ATeachersPrayer?ref=ts&fref=ts

While I was rereading, I noticed that Tammy wept once she found out Jesus died for her. To Tammy, love was only a word that carried no meaning, and this changes my view of everything. I have always had loving parents and friends who show that love is not just a word, but so much more. Because of my experiences, I can not even fathom love being just a word. It also shows that people at shool, church, or wherever are not doing a good enough job of loving. We want to stay in our comfort zones, but Jesus called us to do more. We need to practice radical hospitality and love to the outsider and loner. I need to be an example and try to not worry about what others think. I need to do the right thing and love the outsider and loner.

Written by a 9th grade student, Lewis Purdue, as part of a journal assignment for an autobiography read.

Dear Mr. & Mrs. Brown,

[redacted] I feel like I am going to go home a better and stronger leader. My small group and the conversations I was able to have with them will stay with me and help me prosper as a person. I have realized this week that I have more flaws than I realized and I now understand that ever little giggle and mean look I have ever throw could affect & really hurt someone. Your story in particular has touched me because it was a nice wake up call, and has brought me into the reality of real world situations. I am going to go to school now and go out of my way to stand up for people, give a helping hand, give the grace of God's love, and flash more smiles to people I've never talked to before in the hallways. You have been an absolute inspiration to me and I hope one day someone can remember me as being their "Tiffany". Thank you so much for giving me the knowledge & reminding me that the world isn't all happy, but we can be leaders and set goals to make the world better. [redacted] I have made memories that I will look back at and cherish forever. May God bless both of you and your family.

                                    -Julie Kanan

Print these out and put them in several random places throughout your house, work and/or car to remind you daily to look for ways to show kindness!

Kindness is the language which the deaf can hear and the blind can see.
Mark Twain

"People are often unreasonable and self-centered. Forgive them anyway.
If you are kind, people may accuse you of ulterior motives. Be kind anyway.
If you are honest, people may cheat you. Be honest anyway.
If you find happiness, people may be jealous. Be happy anyway.
The good you do today may be forgotten tomorrow. Do good anyway.
Give the world the best you have and it may never be enough. Give your best anyway.
For you see, in the end, it is between you and God. It was never between you and them anyway."
Kent M. Keith

"For Attractive lips, speak words of kindness.
For lovely eyes, seek out the good in people.
For a slim figure, share your food with the hungry.
For beautiful hair, let a child run their fingers through it once a day.
For poise, walk with the knowledge that you never walk alone.
People, more than things, have to be restored, renewed, revived, reclaimed, and redeemed. Remember, if you ever need a helping hand, you will find one at the end of each of your arms.
As you grow older, you will discover that you have two hands, one for helping yourself and the other for helping others."
Sam Levinson

"The words of the tongue should have three gatekeepers: Is it true? Is it kind? Is it necessary?"
Arabian proverb

"I hope you will have a wonderful year, that you'll dream dangerously and outrageously, that you'll make something that didn't exist before you made it, that you will be loved and that you will be liked, and that you will have people to love and to like in return. And, most importantly (because I think there should be more kindness and more wisdom in the world right now), that you will, when you need to be, be wise, and that you will always be kind."
Neil Gaiman

"You cannot do a kindness too soon, for you never know how soon it will be too late."
Ralph Waldo Emerson

"Few will have the greatness to bend history itself, but each of us can work to change a small portion of events. It is from numberless diverse acts of courage and belief that human history is shaped. Each time a man stands up for an ideal, or acts to improve the lot of others, or strikes out against injustice, he sends forth a tiny ripple of hope, and crossing each other from a million different centers of energy and daring those ripples build a current which can sweep down the mightiest walls of oppression and resistance."
Robert F. Kennedy

"Nothing is so much calculated to lead people to forsake sin as to take them by the hand and to watch over them in tenderness. When persons manifest the least kindness and love to me, O what pow'r it has over my mind."
Joseph Smith, Jr.

www.ingramcontent.com/pod-product-compliance
Lightning Source LLC
Chambersburg PA
CBHW081639040426
42449CB00014B/3377